Pebble Mosaics

Pebble Mosaics

25 original step-by-step projects for the home and garden

DEBORAH SCHNEEBELI-MORRELL
and
GLORIA NICOL

CICO BOOKS

London

For Heini Schneebeli with gratitude for his
encouragement and support

First published in 2002 by Cico Books Ltd
32 Great Sutton Street London EC1V 0NB

Edited by Gillian Haslam
Photography by Gloria Nicol
Styling by Deborah Schneebeli-Morrell
Designed by Roger Daniels

Printed and bound in Singapore by Tien
Wah Press

NOTE ON MEASUREMENTS: The
measurements for each of the projects in the
book are given both in metric and imperial
quantities. Once you have decided which
system to use, do follow it through the
project, as the measurements are not
interchangeable.

Contents

Introduction

The art of pebble mosaics has a long history and some of its ancient methods and traditions are still used today. For example, contemporary pavements and terraces in Greece echo and imitate those of the ancient world; in fact the same kinds of smooth, uncut colored pebbles can still be found and make a remarkably enduring surface when arranged as a mosaic floor. Certain kinds of vernacular architecture are characterized by the type of stone or pebble used – the nearer the sea, the more likely you are to find sea-washed cobbles, while further inland local stones dug out of the earth, such as flints, may be used for their decorative qualities.

This book will give you many inspirational ideas, from the simplest projects such as the border edging on page 32 or lattice planter on page 96 to more complicated larger projects using a combination of textures and materials. These require patience and a little more skill but the results can be spectacular, such as the tree collar on page 18 where pebbles are set into a circular cement base to make a permanent ring around a tree, or the pebble and stone path on page 36 which could transform your garden.

You can collect stones, pebbles or shells from the countryside, but don't take too many and be aware of the environmental effect. With the growing interest in garden design it is now possible to buy inexpensive bags of pebbles in many colors, sizes, textures and forms. Contrast these properties to enhance your design – rough against smooth, dark against light, large against small. Shells also work beautifully with pebbles, as do broken china and flowerpots. Few tools are required and there are no specialized techniques. Simply follow the cement mix recipes exactly for the best results. For all outdoor projects, make sure you use specialist exterior waterproof and frostproof cement or grout. This is generally of professional standard and the type used for tiling swimming pool interiors.

Gallery

LEFT Stone mosaic paths have been used in gardens for centuries. The Mexican artist Frida Kahlo designed her own stepping stone paths, seen here in her Mexico City garden. Following an Art Deco pattern, the central stones are flecked with turquoise, Mexico's national gemstone. The discipline of the stonework contrasts with the lush, tumbling vines and ferns that the artist loved to paint in her youth.

RIGHT A common technique involves creating a graphic image with a design of dark pebbles clearly delineated against a paler background. This works best when pebbles are all of a similar size.

ABOVE Pebbles, stone, gravel and wood are used as a combination that echoes modern Japanese design. The regular lines of the decking against the smooth pebbles create a peaceful feeling of calm.

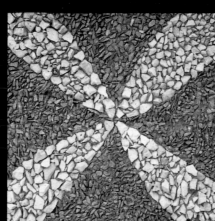

ABOVE The combination of geometric and a more freely drawn design is characteristic of many ancient mosaic terraces or pavements. The fact that many examples of such mosaics still exist today is a tribute to the true durability of pebbles as a paving medium.

ABOVE This simple flower motif is made of stone chips in gray and buff colors. The technique works well for wall decorations but you need patience to assemble all the small pieces.

RIGHT This simple contemporary mosaic is made up of granite setts and white cobbles. The central channel is the base of a stream; the resulting bright green water algae has colored the white pebbles.

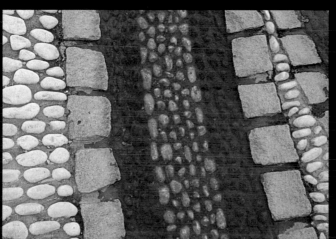

ABOVE Straight lengths of stone divide this pebble mosaic into compartments, emulating the style of a European eighteenth-century parterre.

RIGHT The eccentric combination of paint, china mosaic and cement relief-work is typical of the naive artist's approach to home decor. Broken china is a favored medium, partly because it is often colorful, but, of course it is cost-free and easily available.

RIGHT The outside walls of this house have been covered with broken china mosaic, using colored but plain china pieces in an abstract design, with shells. This is probably a long-term project added to over the years through each summer.

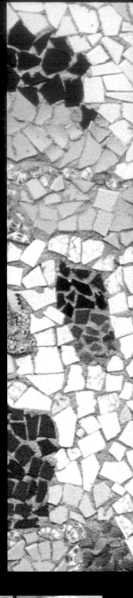

RIGHT This modest little diamond-patterned garden path has no doubt been created by the owner of the house and it is most likely that all the gray and white pebbles were collected locally from a nearby beach.

RIGHT This richly encrusted shell border surrounds the door to a celebrated shell grotto at the royal home of Hampton Court Palace in London. To make this kind of mosaic you will need to build up a large collection of varied shells.

ABOVE A detail from inside the Palace shell grotto shows the framing around a Gothic window. Delightful shell flowers have been cleverly made using the inside of cockle shells. Grottos became very fashionable in Europe during the eighteenth century.

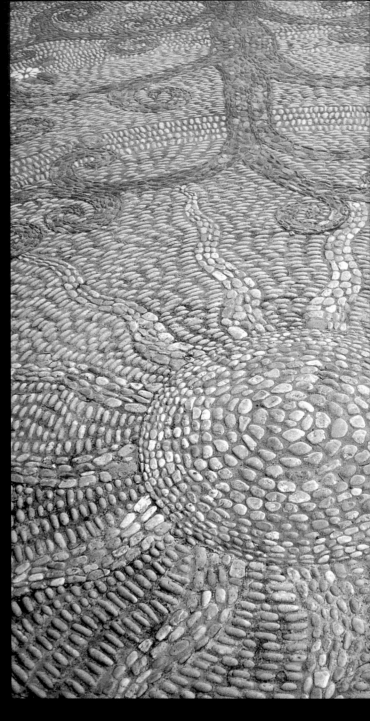

ABOVE Roman mosaics are characterized by their intricate use of pattern, created by cutting marble tessarae to fit. Fortunately, perfect examples of mosaic floors survive all over the former Roman empire. This floor comes from Hadrian's villa at Tivoli in Italy.

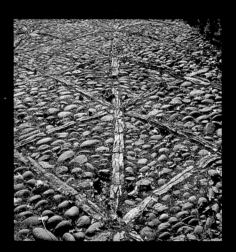

ABOVE The method used in this path is centuries-old; long stones placed on edge make a geometric, dissected diamond pattern. The spaces between stones are tightly filled with uniform pebbles create strength and durability.

LEFT These river pebbles have been laid, rhythmically, into a fish-scale design. All the design here comes from the simple arrangement of the stones; no color or other materials have been added.

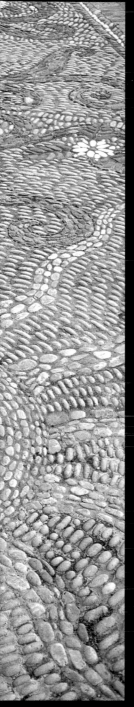

LEFT This contemporary pebble mosaic has been expertly made so that the surface is completely even. The pattern has been enhanced by laying the pebbles in rhythmic forms which makes the path it forms seem almost alive.

RIGHT This detail of the mosaic above shows the curling branches of the stylized tree. The overall design is punctuated by the use of small white pebbles, as in the flower, or studded through the herringbone border.

RIGHT This intricate latticed path runs through the large gardens of the Alhambra Palace in Spain. The herringbone pattern of the lattice manages to create a three-dimensional effect, as the contrasting diamond shapes between are filled in with pale pebbles.

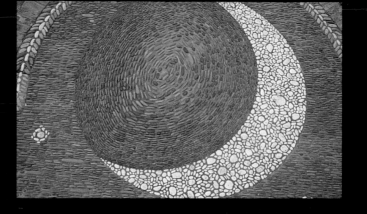

RIGHT Featuring in the same contemporary mosaic as shown in the two photographs directly below, this crescent moon has been made up from different-sized white pebbles. Note how the remaining dark side shows up purely because the dark stones are laid in the rhythm of concentric circles.

ABOVE The pebbles for the fish motif have been selected for their shape and color. Purple slate pieces have been used on the edges of the fish in order to create a linear pattern.

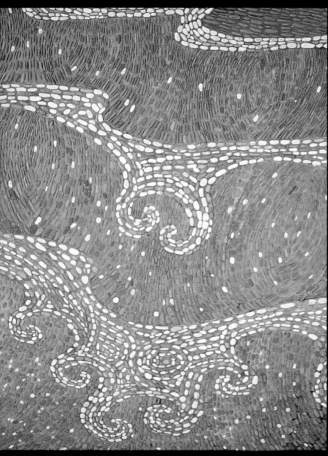

ABOVE This contemporary mosaic has been intricately pieced together. Note how the darker background has been created with elongated pebbles laid on their sharp sides, in deliberate contrast to the flatter white pebbles used to pick out the swirling motifs.

LEFT This stylized portrait by the twentieth-century French artist Jean Cocteau shows how easy it is to draw with pebbles. The darker lines are emphasized with two rows for a bold effect while the paler background is created from randomly placed but, significantly, even-sized pebbles.

Pebble Mosaics • 15

Paths,
Plaques
and
Panels

Mosaic tree collar

Special trees are often planted to mark an important occasion; a walnut planted to celebrate the birth of a child will grow and mature with that child and provide a bounteous crop of nuts to be harvested throughout his or her life. Trees planted in this way hold a particular significance and add a sense of permanence to the garden, reminding us of the continuity of the natural world and that we are part of it. Similarly, a tree planted to commemorate the life of a much-loved person will be a prized tree, an enduring and poignant reminder.

This tree will often be placed thoughtfully in a garden and a magical circular mosaic around its trunk can mark its significance while making an unusual decorative statement. It has a practical use, too, allowing the circle of earth around the base of the tree to be free from encroaching weeds and grass, ensuring the maximum absorption of water and making a generous space for the application of a nourishing mulch and occasional fertilizer.

MATERIALS

- Rope 6ft (2m) long
- 8 metal or wood stakes approximately 12in (30cm) long
- Hammer
- Garden spade
- Red clay tile shards
- Carpenter's level
- Gravel
- Garden rake
- 10 large stones, 3½–4in (8–10cm) in diameter
- River pebbles 1¼–1½in (3–4cm) long
- Larger pebbles 1½–2½in (4–6cm) long
- 1 bucket small white pebbles
- 3 buckets
- Builder's sand
- Cement
- Trowel
- Rubber mallet
- Steel brush

step **1**

Tie the rope around the base of the tree trunk and make a knot 32in (80cm) from the trunk. Walk the rope around the trunk marking the 32in (80cm) radius at eight points. Bang in a stake at each of these points.

step **2**

Use the spade to cut away the marked circle of turf; if you don't feel sufficiently confident to continue the circle by eye between the stakes, use the rope as a guide. An easy way to remove turf is to divide it into spade-sized widths and slice it away from the soil beneath.

step *3*

Along the circle's outer perimeter, set in the red clay tile shards or half tiles to create an edging level with the surrounding grass. Tie another knot in the rope 16in (40cm) from the trunk, and use this to mark the inner circle. Insert the tiles and use a level to check they are pushed into the same depth as the tiles in the outer circle.

step *4*

Fill in between the two circles of tiles with gravel and rake it level so it is approximately 2in (5cm) from the top of the tiles. Tread the gravel down firmly so it is well compacted.

step *6*

You will need to make the mosaic in sections, as there is only a certain amount of time in which to work before the mortar hardens. Mix eight parts sand to one part cement and add water to make a sloppy consistency. Shovel the cement into the circle, on top of the gravel, so it reaches ¾in (2cm) from the top of the tile surround, leveling it roughly with the trowel.

step *5*

Sort out the pebbles into separate buckets, discarding any chipped or misshapen ones and choose ten of the largest variety.

step 7

First position all the large pebbles around the circle equally spaced, and centering them between the tiles. Place the ten stones in the mortar, about 16in (40cm) apart and bang in gently with the rubber mallet so they are half submerged in the mortar.

step 8

Using the larger-sized small pebbles, make a ring around each large stone. You need to build up five concentric rings around each stone banging the pebbles in with the mallet. Set them in so that they are well anchored in the mortar and carefully place them so they fit together well, leaving a minimum of gaps.

step 9

Sort out some of the longer white pebbles and mark out large circles with them by setting them well into the mortar. Make sure the tops are level with all the other pebbles.

step 10

Fill in the spaces within and around the white-ringed circles with smaller pebbles. Try to arrange them in a pattern so they all follow each other. Allow the mortar to dry overnight, then brush away any debris. Unwanted mortar can be brushed away using a steel brush.

Paving slabs

These boldly striped paving slabs are made using the indirect mosaic method, where the design is made in reverse using a square mold. This simple, traditional method means that any number of slabs can be made in comfort, perhaps working on a tabletop rather than crouching on the ground.

The stripes are created using white pebbles set against the rich red ocher of terra cotta shards. If you don't have enough broken flowerpots, most garden centers will have a ready supply which they are only too happy to get rid of. You may even be lucky enough to find pieces of the more fashionable, glazed pots, which can be randomly inserted into your design, injecting a surprising element of color, pattern or texture.

These slabs have been laid in a classic potager design, each one separated from the next by a frame of complementary red bricks. You can, of course, arrange the slabs to make any number of different pattern combinations, in a terrace, or as laid here, as a path surrounding a well-kept vegetable bed.

MATERIALS

- Ready-made frame mold (inner dimensions 12in (30cm) square by 2in (5cm) deep)
- Large bowl of sand
- Bucket of small white pebbles
- Bucket of terra cotta shards
- Tile nippers
- Small amount of green glazed pottery
- White pencil
- Bag of ready-mix sand and cement (or mix one part cement to four parts builder's sand)
- Trowel and bucket
- Piece of chicken wire 11½in (29cm) square
- Small household paintbrush
- Stiff brush

step **1**

Put a thin ⅛in (2-3mm) layer of sand in the base of the frame, spreading it evenly. Keep in mind as you lay the pebbles that you are working from the back—lay pebbles "face" down.

step **2**

Place a row of white pebbles along the central diagonal, laying them down with their flattest side down, facing the sandy base.

step **3**

Use the tile nippers to cut the terra cotta shards into 1¼in (3cm) squares. This is relatively easy to do, as terra cotta is fired at a low temperature and therefore quite brittle. Lay the squares along each side of the diagonal white stripe, shaping the corner pieces to fit.

step **4**

Continue making alternate lines, randomly adding pieces of colored glazed pottery into the terra cotta stripes. Mark these with a white pencil cross on the back of each one so that you know where they are. Finish with a white pebble in opposite corners.

step 6

Lay the piece of chicken wire onto the wet cement and push it in slightly; it helps if the wire is as flat as possible.

step 7

Mix some more cement to a slightly stiffer consistency and fill the rest of the frame. Smooth it off level with the trowel. Put the mold aside to dry for three or four days.

step 5

Mix the cement so that it is sloppy without being too runny. Trowel it into the frame over the design so it reaches halfway up the sides. Work the cement into the gaps between the mosaic pieces by using the edge of the trowel. The further the cement is worked in, the better the grip and the more secure the finished slab will be. The stones should be completely covered.

step 8

Remove the slab from the mold by unscrewing the sides from the base. Turn the slab over, remove it from the base and place it right side up.

step 9

Brush away the sand with a stiff brush. If any of the gaps between the mosaic pieces are too deep, brush a dry mix of one part cement to two parts sand over the slab to fill the gaps (this is best done when the slabs are laid in place). A gentle sprinkling of water from a hose will ensure the powdery cement hardens in place.

Stepping stones

A row of stepping stones in a lush green lawn invites you to follow its path, curving or straight, perhaps, as here, wandering through a maze of glorious spring flowers. The path of stones could lead to a more ambitious pebble terrace, which reflects elements of the star pattern that features on each of the stepping stones themselves.

Highly practical as well as appealing, stepping stones protect your lawn and its surrounding features, as well as allowing you and garden visitors the opportunity to admire your plantings at closer quarters. Stepping stones are also popular placed around a rockery, in an arborium, or meandering through the fragrant drifts of a delicate herbaceous border. Each stone is conveniently spaced so you do not disturb plants while weeding or gathering flowers.

Being small, the stone panels are quick and easy to make. Selected pebbles are cemented in a bold and contrasting design onto a plain circular paving slab (readily available at a low cost from good garden centers). The star design is simple to repeat; you could also personalize your work by placing a different letter on each stone to spell out a name or place along the path.

MATERIALS

- Precast concrete circular paving slabs, approximately 12in (30cm) in diameter
- Large brown pebbles approximately 1½ in (4cm) diameter (pebbles need to be selected from a larger quantity to obtain evenly matching examples)
- White pebbles approximately ½–1in (1.5–2.5cm) (usually bought by the bag)
- Smaller brown flattened river pebbles (usually bought by the bag)
- Frostproof and waterproof gray cement adhesive
- Old kitchen knife

step 1
Sort the pebbles into even sizes. Make sure the brown pebbles you choose are quite flat as they will be used around the edge of each stone.

step 2 (right)
Follow the instructions on the pack to mix the cement adhesive with water. Once it is of a fairly stiff consistency, spread it over the concrete slab. It should cover the whole slab to a depth of around 1/2in (1–1.5cm). Leave a clean border about 1/2in (1.5cm) wide around the edge.

step 3
Mark an eight-pointed star centrally onto the cement with the tip of the old knife. Do not worry if it is uneven – simply rub out the knife marks and start again.

step 4
Choose one of the largest round brown pebbles and place it in the center of the star.

step 5
Push in four white pebbles along each diagonal line. Try to use a pointed pebble facing outward at the end of the line; leave a border 3/4in (2cm) at the end of the slab.

step 6
Now begin to push in the smaller brown river pebbles. Use flatter pebbles, fitting them in on their sides. This makes it easier to fit them at the center. Leave a gap around the edge.

step 7
Coat the backs of slightly larger brown pebbles with adhesive and place them around the edge, pushing well in. Clean off any adhesive that protrudes. Leave to dry overnight.

Border edging

This easy project is surprisingly effective. A readily available precast clay edging has been customized by the simple addition of a double row of river pebbles along the wavy top. It turns an ordinary object into something much more personal. You could even incorporate special stones and give them a permanent place in the garden. The pebbles are transformed by rain or early morning dew, the wetness bringing out the incredible variety and beauty of each pebble, allowing us to see them again as they were in the river.

When planting flowers against the edging, try to consider the color of the pebbles as you choose your plants; leaves with a wine-red tinge or pink and purple flowers seem to work particularly well with the combination of pebble colors used here.

MATERIALS

- Gray cement-based waterproof and frostproof adhesive
- Old pointed kitchen knife
- Container for cement
- Precast wavy border edging
- Pebbles approximately 1¼-1½in (3-4cm) in diameter
- Modeling tool

step 1

Mix the cement according to manufacturer's instructions and apply a thin layer – about ¼in (5mm) – to the top of the edging. Only cover two humps at a time or the cement will begin to dry. Starting at one end, set in a double row of pebbles.

step 2

Continue in this way along the length of the edging, finishing one stone short of the end. This is so the edging strips fit together well (the extra pebbles can be attached when the edging is in place in the garden).

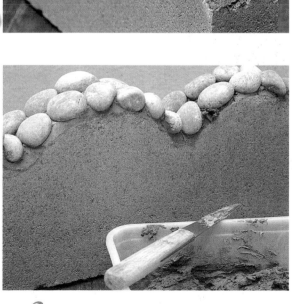

step 3

Clean off the excess cement with the pointed knife, taking care not to get any cement on the sides of the edging strip.

step 4

You can add more cement to the top between the stones to make a neater finish, removing excess with the modeling tool. Allow to dry thoroughly before use.

Pebble and stone garden path

This is a most rewarding project as you can make a huge difference to your garden when you start to design it using hard landscaping. As long as you follow the techniques shown here, it really isn't difficult to do.

The beauty of this path is that many of the stones used were actually dug up in the garden, so what was once a nuisance has become an asset. This is an ages-old method of paving roads in stony areas. Of course, not everybody has access to their own supply of stones and you may have to buy them.

The modular pattern of the path means that it can be used to make a path of any size simply by repeating the elements.

MATERIALS

For one section of the path

- 1 bucket of flat limestone pieces, approximately 3½in (9cm) long and 3in (7.5cm) deep (these will vary greatly in size)
- 1 bucket of pebbles at least 2in (5cm) in length
- Large pebble 3¼in (8cm) long, for the center of the diamond
- Large bag of gravel
- Stiff rake
- Carpenter's level
- Bag of builder's sand
- Bag of waterproof and frostproof cement
- Shovel
- Cement float
- Pointed stick
- Rubber mallet

step *1*

Sort the flat stones into similarly sized pieces and wash them to remove any earth. Sort the pebbles, discarding any smaller than 2in (5cm) across, as smaller pebbles will not anchor well in the cement.

step *2*

Spread the gravel to a depth of about 2in (5cm). Rake it level and tread down to compact it. The edge of this path was previously laid by setting larger pieces of limestone into cement; the even level was obtained by using a carpenter's level.

step *3*

Mix the mortar by adding four parts builder's sand to one part cement. Mix thoroughly and add water, carefully mixing all the time. When it is of a fairly stiff consistency, shovel it into place between the edging stones. Using the float, flatten it out so that it is level (use the carpenter's level or do it by eye). Mark off sections 24in (60cm) square and draw a diamond shape within each square with a pointed stick.

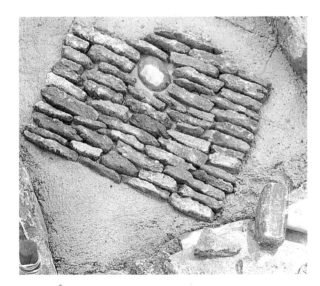

step *5*

Fill in the areas around the stone diamond by setting the pebbles into the mortar on end. Pack them in as tightly as possible and use the mallet to bang them in all to the same level. Leave for a couple of days for the mortar to dry before using. Repeat this process to make the path as long as you like.

step *4*

Set the large pebble into the center of the diamond and start to set the flat stones on their edges all around the center pebble, all pointing in the same direction. Bang them in gently with the mallet. They need to be level, so some will have to be banged in further than others.

Evening table

This pebble mosaic table has been made in an old galvanized greenhouse tray. This acts as a casting mold for the cement base and also creates an ideal solution to the problem of mosaic edges, as pebbles set around these unframed cement edges may be vulnerable and become loose. Four holes have been created along one side of the tabletop set into the geometric checkered design, and are filled with removable pumice-stone tealight holders. When lit with glowing votive candles, they provide a magical evening atmosphere. During the day, the candles can be removed and similar-sized pots of cacti or succulents can be displayed. The plants will love the reflected warmth from the pebble surface. Although this table is heavy, it can be moved around the garden, although it is best suited to a permanent home on a terrace near the house.

MATERIALS

- Builder's sand
- Cement
- Galvanized tray 32×19×3in deep (80×48×8cm deep)
- 5 plastic flowerpots, approximately 5in (12cm) in diameter
- Black pebbles 1–1½in (2.5-4cm) long
- White pebbles 1–1½in (2.5-4cm) long
- River pebbles 1½in (4cm) long
- 4 pumice-stone candle-holders 3in (8cm) deep×4in (10cm) diameter
- Pointed stick

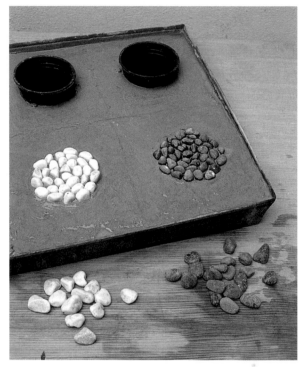

step **1**

Add four parts sand to one part cement and mix thoroughly, then add water to make a fairly stiff consistency. You will need about two large buckets of cement to fill the galvanized tray. Visually divide the tray in half lengthwise and place four plastic flower pots along the side at the back of the tray, equally spaced. Fill the tray with the cement mixture, burying the pots so that only the rims are visible. Use a pointed stick to divide the cement into eight sections and use an upturned flowerpot to mark circles in the center of the four squares along the front of the tray.

step **2**

Fill two of the marked circles on the front section of the tray with black pebbles and two with white pebbles, alternating the colors. Push the pebbles half way into the wet cement.

step **3**

Push the river pebbles half way into the cement all around the edge of the tray and along the marked lines dividing the eight sections of the tray.

Place the tabletop on some mossy bricks or stones so that it is at coffee table height.

step 4

Use white pebbles to fill in the squares around the black circles and the black pebbles to fill in the squares around the white circles. Set the pebbles tightly together, taking care not to squeeze any cement up in between them.

step 5

Fill the squares around the sunken flowerpots with contrasting pebbles to those on the front squares, creating a checkerboard effect. Allow the cement to dry for two days, then gently ease out the plastic pots. Insert the stone candle-holders into the holes left by the plastic pots and place a large tealight in each one.

Garden bench

This regal garden seat looks, and is, a rather an ambitious project, although the technique involved is not at all complicated. The most important quality to have when attempting to make the bench is patience – it will take some time to make, so you could space out the work over a number of weeks, doing a few hours at a time. The sense of achievement you will experience when it is completed will more than make up for the amount of work you have put in.

There are no expensive materials used in the construction of the bench, which is mainly made from broken terra cotta pots. If you don't have enough terra cotta pots on hand, many garden centers will save pieces of the pots from breakages they have. The softness of the terra cotta clay means that the pieces can be cut accurately so you can fit them neatly together, rather than creating an untidy crazy-paving effect. As the base underneath the surface is molded with cement, the finished seat, with its white pebble piping, mimics a real upholstered sofa, making a witty feature for a prominent place in your garden.

MATERIALS

- Bricks
- Cement
- Container for cement
- Piece of chalk
- Cement-based adhesive
- White pebbles approximately 1–1½in (3–4cm) long
- China pieces for flower motifs
- Tile nippers
- White glazed china
- Terra cotta pieces
- Waterproof and frostproof cement-based grout
- Rubber gloves
- Damp cloth

step **2**

Mix the cement adhesive according to manufacturer's instructions. Apply cement to the backs of the white pebbles and stick them along the flower stems in the central design and around the edges of the bench, seat and arms, as in the picture.

step **1**

Build the base and arms of the bench from bricks. Mix the cement and cover and build up the base and the arms, along with the back of the chair, to create the curves that will help to mimic an upholstered piece. When the cement is dry, use the chalk to mark out your design onto the seat, back and arms of the bench.

step **3**

Cut the matt china into petal-shaped pieces using the tile nippers. Some of the petals will be a composite of pieces, especially if your china comes from a bowl with curved sides. Remember that the smaller the china pieces, the flatter the finished surface will be.

step *4*

Cut the white glazed china into leaf shapes with the tile nippers and stick in place at intervals along the white pebble stems. As the china is thinner than terra cotta, which will be used to create the background, you will need to build up the cement behind the china pieces so that they will finish off at roughly the same level as the terra cotta surface.

step *5*

Cut approximately 10 circles from the terra cotta and stick into the center of the flowers by applying a little cement to the back of each circle. Make sure that you don't use too much cement as this will make the circles protrude and complicate the final grouting by leaving an uneven surface.

step *6*

Stick six of the china petals onto each flower. If you are making the bench in stages with time in between, remember to cut away any excess cement as you go. If left to dry, this excess cement will make it difficult to fit new pieces closely against those already in position.

You now need to fill in the background with the pieces of broken terra cotta. Cut each piece as you go making sure that it fits neatly against the next, leaving an even gap of 1/10in (2mm) around each piece for grout. Some of the pots will be of different thicknesses – adjust the amount of cement used on each piece so they are all at the same level. Don't use pieces that are too large, as you need the surface to be as flat as possible for the grouting stage. Mix the grout and, wearing the rubber gloves, apply all over the surface by hand, making sure that it is pushed well into the gaps between the mosaic pieces. Remove the excess grout from the surface using a damp cloth. You may need to do this a number of times, rinsing out the cloth each time.

step *8*

Cover the arms of the chair with terra cotta pieces. Make three circles on the seat using the white pebbles. Within these circles make an eight-pointed star, as in the picture, from the white china used for the leaves. As before, make sure you use enough cement beneath the pieces to ensure that they are at the same level as the terra cotta. Place a white pebble at each of the points of the star.

step *9*

Fill all remaining space on the bench with the terra cotta pieces, covering any remaining visible cement. Cut the pieces carefully with the tile nippers so that they fit together leaving an even 1/10in (2mm) gap around each one. Apply grout to the remaining ungrouted areas as before, removing the excess with a damp cloth. Leave to dry overnight.

Boat panel

This technique of creating a picture by setting shells and pebbles into a cement-plastered surface is much loved by amateur and folk artists all over the world. The technique can even be used to cover a whole house, creating a highly elaborate, decorated surface. Patterned china is a favorite material for artists who use this approach, as it is easily available and often highly colored. The same technique was used when making shell grottos, which became fashionable in the eighteenth century – the walls and ceilings of the grottos were encrusted with thousands of different shells, creating a magical effect.

This project uses elements of the cement plaster render as part of the design, making the finished picture look like a drawing on a background. For more inspiration, refer to books on native or folk art, where you will find many bold and simple images that are suitable for this approach.

tip You need to work fairly quickly while the cement is still soft enough to set the pebbles and shells in easily.

MATERIALS

- Selection of large and small shells
- Selection of small pebbles
- Builder's soft sand
- Cement
- Bucket for cement
- Wooden board 18 × ½in (45 × 1cm)
- Metal grout float
- Plastic grout float
- Knife (or other pointed object)

step 1

Sort out the shells and pebbles that you wish to use and wash them to remove any dirt.

step 2

Mix four parts sand to one of cement with water, making sure the mixture is not too stiff or too runny. You will need at least one bucket of the mixture. Dampen the wall you wish to render. Place some of the mixture onto the wooden board, then lift a small amount of the mixture with the metal grout float and spread it against the wall – ⅖in (1cm) thick is an ideal thickness. You may have to achieve this in two steps, building up ⅕in (5mm) at a time.

step 3

Allow the rendered cement about 30 minutes to harden very slightly before smoothing the surface with the plastic grout float. This is not strictly necessary, but helps to create a level and smooth surface on which to work.

step 4

Use a pointed object, such as a knife, to draw your design freehand into the surface of the cement render. Copy the design of a simplified sailboat and a ribbon-like border shown on page 51, or you can seek inspiration from naive folk art images to create your own design. Don't worry if the drawing is not perfect as idiosyncrasies will add to the charm of the design.

step 5

Set three rows of mussel shells (each row facing a different way) into the cement, a little distance underneath the boat to suggest waves. Set them deep enough into the cement so that they have a firm grip.

step 6

Create the hull of the boat by studding the area with small, evenly shaped pebbles. The pebbles should be set halfway into the cement to ensure that they have a firm grip. Set in a row of long, pointed shells to delineate the top of the hull, extending them over the edge on the right side of the boat to show the deck.

step **7**
Make the masts out of cowrie shells and top each one with a pointed shell. Fill in the sails with small mauve-tinted shells with their open sides down.

step **8**
Create the ribbon band around the design by setting cowrie shells and smaller black shells alternately along the ribbon line.

Sundial

Placing a sundial in a sunny part of the garden increases awareness of the position of the sun in the sky at different times in the year and therefore the shortening and lengthening of the days. This is of great importance to a gardener, who needs to know how much sunlight reaches each part of the garden at certain times, in order to decide which plants to plant where. A sundial could be a major feature of the garden, positioned perhaps at the end of a path or as a center to a mosaic terrace.

This is a relatively easy project, as the mosaic design has been created on a ready-made sundial bought from a garden center. The sun motif is made from small pieces of purple slate and small river pebbles surrounded by small black shells. The markers that represent the hours are white shells placed among the pebble border.

MATERIALS

- Waterproof and frostproof cement-based adhesive
- Container for cement
- Small pointed kitchen knife
- Metal sundial 12in (30cm) diameter
- River pebbles 1in (2.5cm) long
- Purple slate pieces between 1in (2.5cm) and 2in (5cm) long
- Chalk
- Black shells ½in (1.5cm) to 1in (2.5cm) long
- 9 white shells 1in (2.5cm) long

step **1**

Mix up the cement to a fairly stiff consistency and use the knife to spread a circle of cement ⅖in (1cm) deep around the pointer of the sundial.

step **2**

Set the river pebbles into the cement in concentric circles around the pointer of the sundial, making sure they fit tightly together.

step 3

Use the cement, spreading it to a depth of ⅖in (1cm), to make an eight-pointed star shape around the sundial, as in the picture. Set in the slate pieces so that they radiate out from the center of the sundial, forming the points of the stars. With chalk, mark one point at the tip of the pointer and four points on either side of the pointer to mark the hours, as in the picture. These eight points represent 3 hours in the day. You can make these marks accurate by positioning the sundial so that the pointer points due north at midday, then marking where the shadow falls at each hour until you have four points before and four points after midday.

step 4

Fill in the gaps between the points of the star with more cement. Set the small black shells into these areas, making sure that they are as tightly packed as possible, with little cement showing between.

step 5

Finish by making a border around the edge with river pebbles, placing a white shell on each of the chalk points that mark the hours. Leave to dry overnight.

Bee plaque

The bee is a very welcome and necessary visitor to the garden and we are always glad to see the first ones arrive just in time to fertilize the fruit blossoms.

The stylized bee motif used here has been made using broken china surrounded with a rhythmic pattern of pebbles. The body segments are made up using parts of the rim of a yellow bowl and shiny black pebbles, while the veining on the wings has been achieved by using frostproof and waterproof black grout to fill in the gaps between the white china pieces. The broken china used here has been saved from kitchen accidents, but so little is used, it is quite acceptable to break some especially for the project. The whole piece is created in a large, shallow terra cotta saucer, which could be fixed onto a wall or inlaid into a path or terrace.

MATERIALS

- Shallow terra cotta saucer 16in (40cm) diameter
- Piece of chalk
- Rim of yellow china bowl
- Tile nippers
- 6 shiny black pebbles
- Waterproof and frostproof cement-based adhesive
- Container for cement
- Blue/gray patterned china
- White china pieces
- Pebbles approximately 1in (2.5cm) long
- Approximately 40 larger pebbles 1¼in (3cm) long, for the edge
- Waterproof and frostproof black grout
- Waterproof and frostproof dark gray grout
- Small pointed knife
- Damp cloth

step **1**

Draw the outline of the bee freehand onto the terra cotta saucer with chalk.

step **2**

Cut the yellow china rim with the tile nippers into pieces the same width as the body of the bee. Place these pieces along the body alternating them with three upright black pebbles. Finish at the tail end with a pointed black pebble and place two round black pebbles at the head end. After you have laid the pieces out apply cement, mixed according to manufacturer's instructions, to the back of each piece and stick in place.

step 3

Using the tile nippers, cut up the blue/gray patterned china into pieces that fit together as if in a jigsaw and lay in place on the upper wings. Do the same with the white china pieces on the lower wings. Cut the pieces so that there is an even gap around each one to produce a veined effect.

step 4

Cover the area of the upper and lower wings with cement and stick the pre-cut pieces in place. In order to create a level surface, build up cement on the underside of the china pieces you are using here, adding more than you use on the pebbles, as the china will be thinner than the yellow rim or the pebbles.

step 5

Create the bee's antennas with strips of white china topped with a yellow oval end, cut from the yellow bowl. Stick in place with cement as before.

step 6

Spread cement onto the area surrounding the bee motif and set in the smaller pebbles closely together. Arrange the pebbles in circles, following the shape of the edge of the china mosaic to create a rhythmic pattern. Fill in the remaining space on the terra cotta saucer, possibly leaving room for a border.

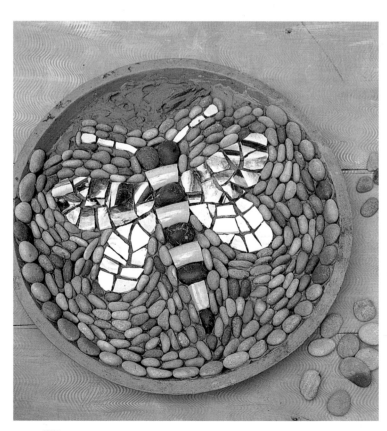

step 7

Create a border around the rim of the terra cotta saucer with larger pebbles.

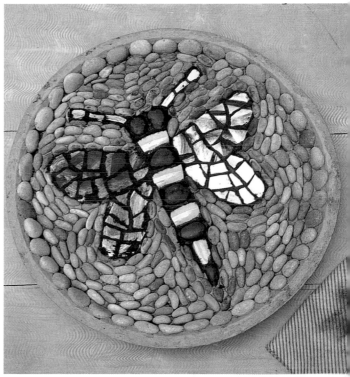

step *8*

Mix the black grout and apply to the bee motif, pushing the grout well into the gaps between the pieces with the small knife. Clean off the excess with a damp cloth. Mix some dark gray grout and apply to the pebble background. Wipe off excess with a damp cloth – this may need to be done a number of times with a rinsed cloth.

tip If unwanted grout remains on the pebbles, it can be brushed off with a wire brush once the grout has dried.

Pebble slab with house motif

The technique used for making this pebble slab is called the indirect method and is often employed when making mosaics. It is known as the indirect method because the design is made upside down – what is placed first in the frame will become the image on the slab. This method is particularly useful when using uneven pebbles, as the finished surface will be very regular. It is very satisfying to place the pebbles into the thin layer of sand, gradually working out your design as you go.

The motif for this project has been taken from a familiar folk art patchwork design. Similar slabs could be made using other iconic images, such as birds, trees or flowers. They would make a unique terrace laid together "patchwork" fashion in a sunny place in the garden.

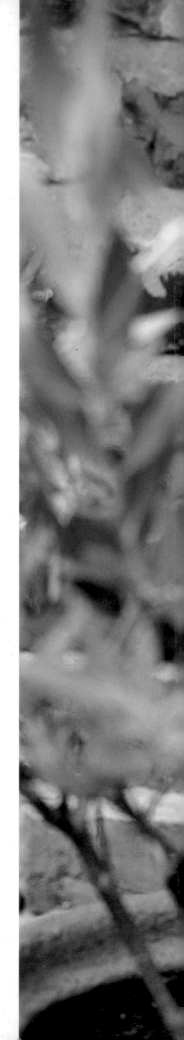

MATERIALS

- Soft sand
- Frame to make slab 12in (30cm) square
- Pointed knife
- Selection of pebbles in black, white and duck-egg blue colors
- Cement
- Container for cement
- Trowel
- Chicken wire 12in (30cm) square
- Stiff brush

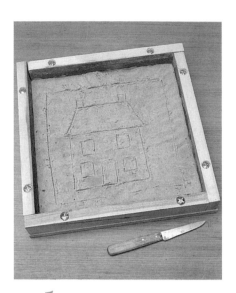

step **2**

Select the pebbles, choosing ones that are as flat as possible to ensure they fit together better. Set pairs of white pebbles into the sand to make the windows and door of the house. Surround these with black pebbles, working symmetrically, to create the front wall of the house. Continue until the front wall of the house is completed.

step **1**

Sprinkle sand evenly into the assembled frame, to a depth of ⅜in (8mm). Press it down firmly and draw your design – in this project a house – into the sand with the point of the knife.

step **3**

Lay several rows of white pebbles horizontally into the sand to make the roof. Use contrasting black pebbles to make the two chimneys.

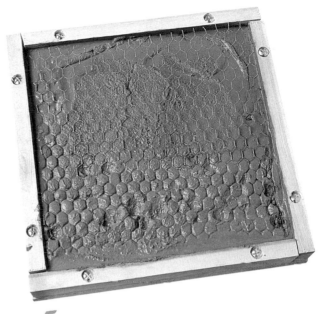

step 4

Surround the house with the blue pebbles, setting them tightly together. Finish the design by surrounding these blue pebbles with a border of black pebbles, also packed closely together.

step 5

Mix three parts sand to one part cement, adding water to make a fairly sloppy consistency. Trowel into the frame and tap with the sharp edge of the trowel at the cement, working it down evenly between the pebbles, and taking care not to dislodge the design. When the cement is ⅘in (2cm) thick, press the chicken wire into the cement for extra strength and fill the frame with the rest of the cement mixture. Trim the wire to fit. Level the surface and set aside to harden for three days.

step 6

Unscrew the frame to release the slab. Turn over and brush away sand stuck between the pebbles. If necessary, you can spray the surface with a jet of water to clear away all traces of the sand.

Number plaque

This novel idea for a house number plaque is created by using a china plate as a background on which to stick the broken china and painted pebble decoration. The plaque is then hung on an outside wall, attached with a conventional wire plate-hanger in the same way you would display an antique or decorative plate. The lead-strip bow makes a witty allusion to this custom and is simply made by bending a strip of lead into shape. The advantage of attaching the number to your house in this way means that you can take it with you if you move, or you can move it to a different location on the wall or door if necessary.

If your house has a name, you can design the plaque, spelling out the name by writing each letter on a different pebble. The pale green broken-china mosaic surrounding the central painted pebble is made from a favorite mug which has been broken, but this transformation means it has a new life.

MATERIALS

- Large oval flat stone, approximately 2 × 2½in (5 × 6cm)
- Sharp pencil
- No. 2 artist's paintbrush
- White acrylic paint
- Frostproof and waterproof gray cement-based adhesive
- Container for cement
- China plate with a wavy edge, 8in (20cm) in diameter
- Tile nippers
- Broken china
- Frostproof and waterproof white or pale gray grout
- Old pointed kitchen knife
- Cloth
- 18 round black pebbles, ¾in (2cm) in diameter
- Wire plate hanger

step **1**

Find a number in a typography book or from your computer in a typeface you like and print or photocopy it to the right size for your chosen stone. Cut out the number, place onto the stone and trace around it with a sharp pencil.

step **2**

Mix the paint with a little water and paint very neatly between the pencil lines. Allow the paint to dry.

step 3

Mix the gray cement according to manufacturer's instructions. Spread liberally onto the back of the pebble and set in place in the center of the plate.

step 4

Use the tile nippers to cut the china into small pieces, then place the pieces jigsaw-like around the pebble until they reach the inside rim of the plate; do this by applying small amounts of cement to the back of each piece. You can use the tile nippers to cut the pieces to fit more closely if necessary.

step 5

Leave the cement to dry for a couple of hours so the china pieces are firmly attached. Mix the grout with a little water until it is a stiff paste, then push it into all the gaps between each piece. Leave to harden very slightly and then rub off the excess with a barely damp cloth. After 30 minutes polish with your fingertips to remove any film that may remain.

step 6

Attach the row of black pebbles at the edge of the circle, hiding the join beneath each pebble. Clean off any protruding cement with the point of the knife. Allow to dry overnight before attaching the plate to a wire plate hanger.

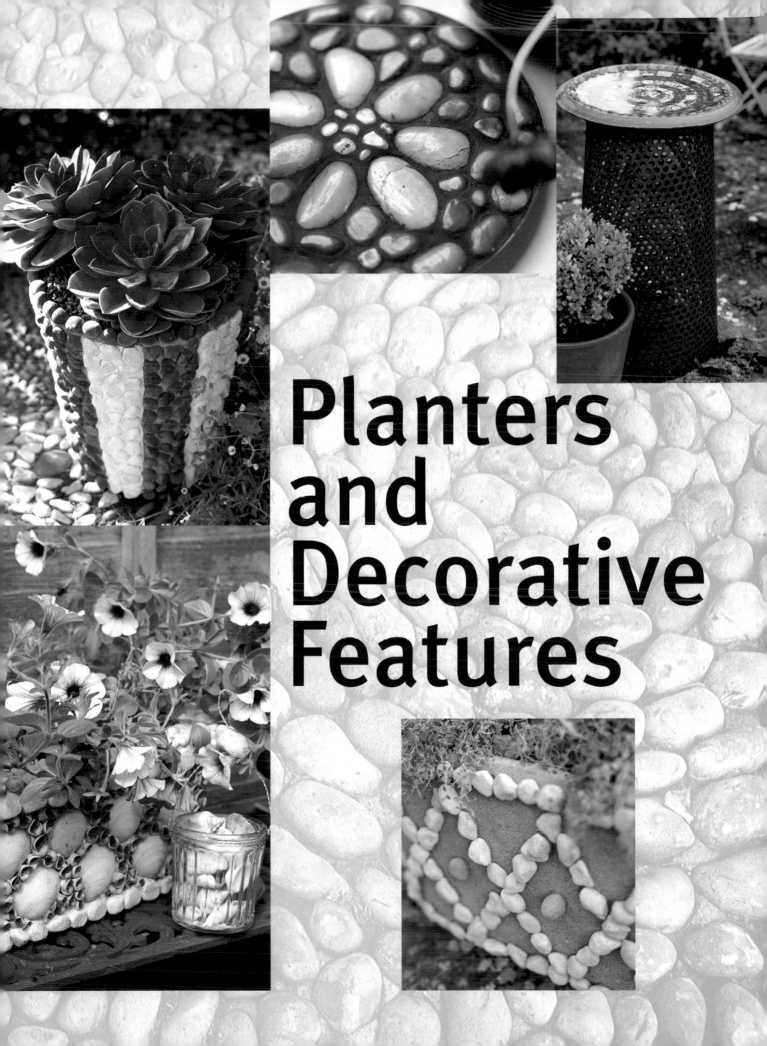

Planters and Decorative Features

Terra cotta plinth

The pale-colored terra cotta plinth, with its barley-twist column, is an object that lends itself perfectly to the art of pebble mosaics. The alternating duck-egg blue and black stones fit snugly into the recesses of the twist design and bands of pebbles of the same colors frame the design at the top and base of the plinth. You may not be able to obtain a plinth identical to the one shown, but you could easily adapt this project to suit a similar one.

This terra cotta plinth can be quite a quick mosaic project to make, but the trick lies in sorting the pebbles into piles of different colors and sizes beforehand. Try to use the flattest pebbles you can find, as these will fit neatly against the terra cotta without protruding too far and distorting the overall shape of the column.

MATERIALS

- Terra cotta plinth approximately
  28in (70cm) high
- Black pebbles approximately
  1in (2.5cm) long
- Duck-egg blue pebbles approximately
  1in (2.5cm) long
- Cement-based frostproof and
  waterproof adhesive
- Container for cement
- Palette knife

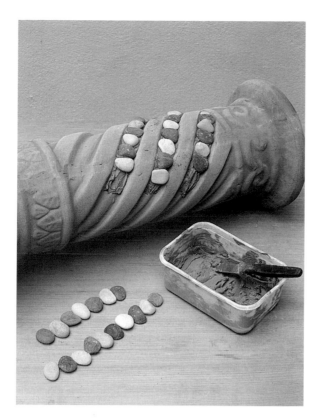

step 1

Sort the pebbles by selecting the flattest and most evenly sized. It helps to arrange them in rows, alternating between the black and duck-egg blue pebbles, so that you know that you will have enough of each color. Mix the cement to a fairly stiff consistency and spread it along each groove in the column to an even depth of about ¼in (5mm). Set the pebbles into place, close together, alternating the colors as you go.

step 2

Spread cement to a depth of ¼in (5mm) in a ring around the base of the column and stick two rings of the flat blue pebbles within the raised frame. Again, the pebbles should be set close together.

step 3

Using the same method, set three rows of the flat black pebbles beneath the two blue rows, within the raised terra cotta frame. Finish by making a band of two rows of the blue pebbles at the top of the column. Allow the cement to dry thoroughly over 24 hours before using the plinth outside.

Pebble Mosaics • 79

Birdbath

This creative project ingeniously makes use of found objects such as broken pieces of willow-pattern china and pebbles gathered on a walk along the beach. These are then arranged in a pattern of concentric circles into a shallow, frostproof terra cotta saucer. Normally sold for use under a large flowerpot, the saucer holds plenty of water to tempt local birdlife, and the use of waterproof cement makes this very durable project a source of admiration for humans and garden guests alike!

When filled with water, the china sparkles brightly and the wet pebbles take on the rich gleam of those found on a wave-washed shore. The traditional blue- and-white plate fragments used here contrast beautifully with the deep purple-brown beach pebbles.

Gathering the materials for this beautiful garden feature could not be easier. Pebbles are now easily available in home decor stores as well as found in the natural surroundings of country places. This is also a wonderful way to give new life to much-loved china that has met with a kitchen accident.

MATERIALS

- Cement-based frostproof and waterproof adhesive
- Container for adhesive
- Shallow terra cotta saucer, 16in (40cm) in diameter
- Tile nippers
- Blue-and-white china pieces
- River pebbles 1in (2.5cm) long
- Modeling tool
- Damp cloth

step 1

Mix the adhesive to a fairly stiff consistency and apply a 4in (10cm) circle to the center of the saucer base. Use the tile nippers to cut out a circle from the china, with a diameter of approximately 1½in (4cm).

step 2

Set the china circle in the adhesive and surround it with a circle of pebbles. Set them halfway into the cement, tightly against the china circle.

step 3

Cut a number of wedge-shaped pieces of china and fit them neatly around the pebble ring, allowing the adhesive to squeeze up a little in between the pieces.

step 4

Surround the circle of china wedges with two concentric rows of pebbles, pushed tightly together.

step 5

Continue with another row of wedge-shaped china pieces, followed by three rows of pebbles. Add another row of china, set so that the pieces are curved slightly inward to follow the mold of the edge of the saucer. Stick a final circle of pebbles around this and fill any spaces with more cement. Allow the cement to harden slightly, then remove any excess with a modeling tool. Remove excess cement from the surface of the china pieces and wipe clean with a damp cloth.

Bubbling fountain

You don't need a large garden to have the pleasure of hearing the gentle sound of water playing over stones. A small space, perhaps even the corner of a small terrace, would be large enough in which to place this pretty white pot which features a small fountain. There are many advantages to containing a fountain within a pot; it is raised off the ground making it more of a visible feature, it creates a focal point and it can also be surrounded by other complementary pots filled with interesting plants – perhaps those that enjoy an occasional splash of water.

There are many affordable small water pumps on the market suitable for this project – many are adjustable, so that you can choose the height of the fountain of water. In this project the pump is adjusted so that the water gently bubbles over the top of the purple slate and river pebbles.

MATERIALS

- Purple slate pieces, assorted sizes
- Round concrete slab 14 in (35cm) in diameter, 1½ in (4cm) thick with a ¾in (2cm) hole in the center. This slab can be precast to fit into the top of the pot; you can also use a standard-sized round cement paving slab and drill a ¾in (2cm) hole in the center. This, and pots to fit, are readily available from garden centers.
- Cement-based adhesive
- Container for cement
- Flat pebbles, assorted sizes
- White glazed pot with rim, 18in (45cm) high, 15in (38cm) diameter and a hole in the base
- Small water pump
- Silicone (to seal hole in base of pot)
- Palette knife
- Bricks

step **1**

To create the top of the fountain, sort the pieces of slate into two piles – one group of longer, thicker pieces and one group of smaller, thinner pieces. Mix the cement according to manufacturer's instructions, and spread a circle of cement approximately 9in (22cm) in diameter and ¾in (2cm) deep around the hole in the center of the round concrete slab.

step **2**

Set four of the larger slate pieces upright into the cement making a cross shape. Make sure that they are clear of the hole in the center.

step **3**

Add more of the larger slate pieces, until there are enough upright pieces in place to create a solid circle. The positioning of the slate pieces should now resemble a star shape. Make sure there is still a clear hole to the bottom of the pot.

step **5**

Cover the part of the round slab that is still visible with cement, ensuring it reaches the edges. Set the flat pebbles into place, radiating out from in and around the circle of slate pieces. Continue adding pebbles until the slab is completely covered. Keep some pebbles back to be used in the final step of the project. Allow the cement to dry overnight.

TO ASSEMBLE THE WATERPUMP

Assemble the pump and place into the pot with the power cable exiting through the hole in the base of the pot. Seal this hole with the silicone, using the palette knife, and allow to set. Build up a firm structure of bricks around the pump so that they are 1½in (4cm) below the rim – this secures the pump in place and provides a base for the fountain top to sit on.

Fill the pot ⅔ full with water. Lower the fountain top slab onto the bricks so that the fountain part of the pump pokes up through the central hole. The slab should be flush with the rim of the pot. Loosely place some more pebbles around the top to disguise the center gap and turn the pump on ready for use.

ALWAYS FOLLOW SAFETY INSTRUCTIONS
WHEN INSTALLING ELECTRIC PUMPS.

step **4**

Set the smaller pieces of slate in between the fixed larger pieces, until the shape resembles the gills on the underside of a mushroom. The slate needs to be packed tightly so that no cement is visible.

Shell windowbox

It seems quite natural to combine seashells and pebbles into a design, as they both originate from the sea or river. Many people have collections of shells, perhaps from as far back as their own childhood, and it is fun to spend many hours sorting them out by color, shape and pattern. Shells are particularly fascinating, as there is an infinite number of varieties, and when you work closely with them, selecting and combining them into an interesting and decorative project such as this pretty windowbox, you will come to know and love them even more.

Luckily it is very easy to buy washed and sorted quantities of inexpensive shells from importers. The larger, clam-shaped shells used here are wonderfully bleached and look as if they have been collected from a sun-drenched beach. The smaller spiral shells have exquisite mauve interiors revealed by using them with the inside facing out.

MATERIALS

- 1lb (500g) white cement-based waterproof and frostproof adhesive
- Palette knife
- Container for cement
- 16 white shells approximately 2¾in (7cm) across
- Terra cotta windowbox approximately 12in (30cm) long, 6in (15cm) high, and 5in (14cm) wide
- Approximately 4½lb (2kg) mauve-lined shells, ½-¾in (1-2cm) in diameter
- Chalky white pebbles approximately ¾in (2cm) in diameter
- Pointed kitchen knife
- Paintbrush

step 1

Mix the cement to a stiff consistency. Arrange and stick the larger white shells onto one side of the windowbox by spreading the adhesive onto the back of the shells and setting them face down into place, four along the top and three beneath (see left). Carefully trim off any excess cement.

step 2

Fill in around the larger shells with small mauve shells, applying a little cement to the pot and a little to the shell itself. Place the shells as close together as you can so little cement will be seen. Complete the front of the box, leaving a strip at the top and base where the white pebbles will go.

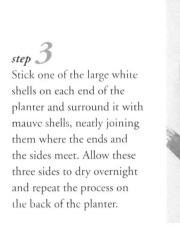

step 3

Stick one of the large white shells on each end of the planter and surround it with mauve shells, neatly joining them where the ends and the sides meet. Allow these three sides to dry overnight and repeat the process on the back of the planter.

step 4

Select white pebbles that have a slightly flattened back. Spread adhesive onto each one separately and set into place along the top and base rims all around the planter. Remove any excess cement with the pointed knife before it hardens.

step 5

Stick a double row of the mauve shells, this time the "right way" up, all around the top of the rim. Remove any excess cement as before. To make a really neat finish, go over the cement with a small damp paintbrush, taking care not to spread any cement onto the shells as it is impossible to remove once dry.

Striped planter

A simple, slightly tapered terra cotta pot has been transformed into a striking planter that could be the focal point of a hot and dry planting scheme. The clean lines of the black and white pebble stripes work particularly well with the strong shapes of sun-loving plants such as *Agave*, *Echiveria* or *Sedum*, lending a Mediterranean feel to your garden. Try decorating other planters and pots in a similar way, perhaps using a slightly different pattern to make an interesting collection to liven up your sunny terrace or patio.

Waterproof and frostproof gray cement has been used for the black pebbles and white cement used for the white ones. Although a little more time-consuming, it is well worth using the two colors as it enhances the black and white contrast. The rim of the pot has been finished with a row of black pebbles that cleverly hide the terra cotta beneath.

MATERIALS

- Tall terra cotta pot 14in (32cm) high with a top diameter of 11in (27cm)
- Piece of chalk
- Black pebbles no more than ¾in (2cm) in diameter
- White pebbles of a similar size
- Waterproof and frostproof gray cement-based adhesive
- Waterproof and frostproof white cement-based adhesive
- Old pointed kitchen knife
- Container for cement

step **1**

Draw vertical chalk lines onto the pot, dividing it into 12 stripes each roughly 3¼in (8cm) wide at the top. On a tapered pot the stripes will be slightly narrower at the base.

step **2**

Mix the gray cement according to manufacturer's instructions, making sure it is not too runny. Apply a layer ½in (1cm) thick within the chalk lines of one stripe and set in the black pebbles closely together. This will push the cement up between the pebbles and help to secure them. Leave room for a row of pebbles around the top rim. Cut off any excess cement with the knife. Leaving the next stripe clear, make two more black stripes.

step **3**

Mix and apply the white cement in the same way between the black stripes and set in the white pebbles. Clean up the joint between each contrasting stripe and continue until one side of the pot is covered. Allow the cement to harden overnight and repeat the same process on the remaining six stripes. It is best to work on the pot in two separate halves so as not to dislodge any pebbles (the pot needs to rest on its side for ease of working).

step **4**

Stand the pot up on its base and stick a row of black pebbles around the upper rim, spreading the back of each pebble with the cement. When the cement starts to harden slightly, trim off any excess with the knife. Allow to harden thoroughly before planting.

tip Don't allow the pebbles to extend beyond the base of the pots. Stop just short, or the bottom row of pebbles will be vulnerable to breaking off and the pot may not be very stable.

Lattice planter

The simulated stone planter used in this project is readily available from garden centers and is perfectly suited as a planter for alpines. A terra cotta planter would work equally well. The simple lattice-work decoration is created by carefully cementing on buff-colored stone chips; these are inexpensive and are usually used for covering paths and driveways. Small round pebbles have been placed in the center of the lattice diamonds.

When filling the planter, remember not to plant anything that would smother the sides and cover up the decoration. Aromatic, low-growing thymes have been selected here. Place the finished planter in an accessible place in the garden, perhaps on a sunny wall at just the right height so that when you brush past the aromatic fragrance of thyme will be released into the summer air.

MATERIALS

- Simulated stone planter approximately 16 × 12in (40 × 30cm) and 7in (18cm) deep
- Piece of white chalk
- Bag of stone chips
- 6 small round pebbles
- Waterproof and frostproof gray cement-based adhesive
- Small pointed kitchen knife

step **1**

Draw the lattice design onto the planter in chalk. There should be three diamonds on the front and back and one on each side. Mark the center of each diamond.

step **2**

Select similarly sized stone chips. Mix the cement and apply a small quantity to the back of each stone. Stick the stones around the top and base of the planter on the front and along the two side edges.

step **3**

Stick the stones in place for the latticework pattern on the front and the sides, ensuring that no cement protrudes from behind them.

step **4**

Stick the round pebbles in the center of each diamond, then leave the cement to set overnight before repeating the design on the back of the planter. Allow the cement to harden thoroughly before planting.

Cube planter

This is an ideal project on which to practice and improve your mosaic skills. Although simple, the finished result is unusual and strikingly effective. The sides of the cube planter are made up of a selection of broken pieces of china, each one a different shade of yellow, creating a subtle and interesting surface. The addition of the rows of small black pebbles along the edges of the cube shape adds to the design, as well as cleverly covering the sometimes messy edges where the sides of appliquéd china meet.

It is helpful to think about which plant you wish to feature in this planter before choosing the colors that you will use. You can then use colored china to complement the color of the intended flower or shade of leaf. You may even like to include a central motif on each side of the planter. It is possible to use this technique on any shaped planter or pot, but keep in mind that the simpler the shape, the easier the technique and more effective the final result will be.

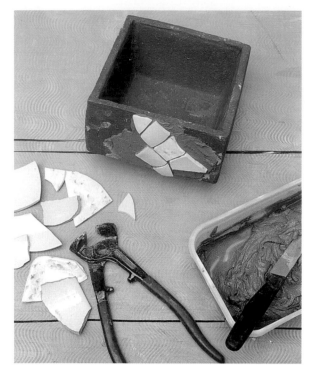

MATERIALS

- Tile nippers
- Assorted pieces of yellow (or other chosen color) china
- Cement-based adhesive
- Container for cement
- Square clay planter 6×6in (15×15cm) ×4in (10cm) deep
- Waterproof and frostproof cement-based gray or white grout
- Palette knife
- Cloths
- Small black pebbles approximately ¾in (2cm) long
- Small pointed kitchen knife

step **1**

Use the tile nippers to cut the china into small pieces. Mix up the cement adhesive according to the manufacturer's instructions and spread onto one side of the planter, covering a small area at a time. Set the selected pieces of china into the cement fixing them close together, again covering a small area at a time. To avoid a crazy-paving effect, cut each piece so that it fits snugly against the next. You will need to add more cement to the back of the thinner pieces so that, when set into place, they form a surface level with the thicker pieces.

step **2**

Continue in the same manner, piecing together a patchwork of varying shades of colored china. Cover each side, stopping just short of all edges, thus leaving space in which to fit the pebbles. Leave to dry overnight.

step **3**

Mix the grout following the manufacturer's instructions and press into all the gaps between the china pieces with the palette knife. Wipe over the surface of the china with a damp cloth and, when dry, polish with a dry cloth.

step **4**

For the edges of the planter, select round pebbles with a flattened side. Add a little cement adhesive to the flat side before setting them into place along the four side edges of the planter.

step **5**

Turn the planter upside down and continue adding the pebbles along the base edges in the same manner as the side edges. Allow the cement to harden overnight before turning the planter the right way up and adding the pebbles around the rim. Allow the cement to begin to harden slightly before removing any excess with the pointed knife.

Pebble basket

This charming little basket is made from flat, elongated pebbles which, when assembled into the basket shape, cleverly mimic the texture of weaving. It is designed to stay outside permanently and could contain a drought-tolerant plant such as *Sedum*. The basket needs to be planted in a modest, unshowy way so that the subtle colors of the chalky gray pebbles can be seen to advantage. When it rains, however, the colors alter, becoming richer and more differentiated, reminding us perhaps of where the pebbles were first found, on the shoreline or in the shallow waters of a gently lapping river.

The basket will need to be made over a couple of days in order to allow the main body to harden slightly before adding the arched handle. Although the cement adhesive used is particularly strong and is even frostproof, it is not advisable to lift the basket by the handle due to the sheer weight of the pebbles.

MATERIALS

- Scissors
- 2 plastic flowerpots approximately 3½in (8cm) in diameter
- Pencil
- Piece of ½in (10mm) thick plywood 10in (25cm) square
- Jigsaw
- 8 flat-headed tacks
- Hammer
- Plastic film
- Gray waterproof and frostproof cement-based adhesive
- Piece of small-gauge chicken wire 10in (25cm) square
- Wirecutters
- Approximately 220 flat gray pebbles 1½in (4cm) longer than wider
- Palette knife
- Container for cement
- Modeling tool
- Paintbrush
- Masking tape

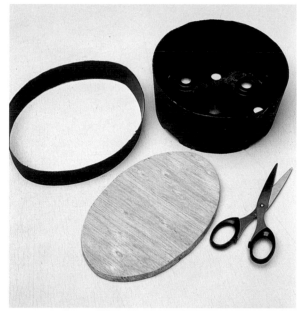

step 1

Use the scissors to cut off the top 1in (2.5cm) of the plastic pot. Squash the pot sides gently to create an oval ring. Place the ring on the plywood, trace the shape and cut out the wood using the jigsaw.

step 2

Push the plastic ring over the plywood oval and secure in place with the eight tacks around the edge of the plywood, equally spaced.

step 3

Place a piece of plastic film into the mold, letting the film drape over the side. Mix the cement adhesive to a creamy consistency and spread in the mold over the plastic film to a depth of about ½in (12mm). Cut the chicken wire to fit and push down into the cement.

step 4

Spread a small amount of adhesive onto the back of each pebble and set into place so that the whole base is covered with pebbles. Leave to set overnight in a cool dry place.

step 5

Remove the plastic ring and lift the cement base from the plywood. Carefully turn it over and remove the plastic film.

step 6

Start to build up the walls of the basket by sticking the first row of pebbles along the perimeter of the oval base. It is best to apply the cement adhesive directly to the back of the pebbles.

step 7

Build up each row in the same manner, placing the pebbles so that they straddle the ones directly underneath. This creates the outward-sloping basket shape.

tip If you want to have plants in the basket, leave a couple of gaps between the lower stones for drainage.

step **8**

After building about five rows, allow the cement to harden slightly by leaving it to stand for 30 minutes. If the sides seem unstable, prop them up by resting mugs against them. At this point you will need to clean up the excess cement before it hardens. Do this by pushing it in with the modeling tool and then removing the excess; a lightly dampened paintbrush will make a neat finish.

step **9**

Apply two more layers of flat stones, finishing off with a row of round pebbles. Leave a space for a flat pebble in the center of each of the long sides (for the handle). Clean off the excess cement and leave to harden for one hour.

step **10**

Cut two more rings of the same size from a plastic flowerpot and tape together to make the ring more rigid. Push the ring into the middle of the basket so that it partly protrudes, making a form for the handle. Carefully build up the handle with flat pebbles, adding slightly more cement between each one. Build up from both sides at the same time, adding the final pebble in the middle of the handle. Allow the cement to begin to harden and clean excess off carefully. The plastic can be carefully removed after a couple of hours and the inside of the handle cleaned.

Nature tray

This white marble display tray with its white pebble edge is one of the simplest and most relaxing projects in this book. With all the qualities of a still life, it is an ideal surface on which to display bleached objects from the natural world, such as coral, shells, white stones, dried seedpods or driftwood. Place it permanently on a garden table, adding or changing the display as you find new and interesting pieces, rather like a living, changing piece of art.

The marble disc used here is a found object. Similar ones in marble or alabaster can be found in home-decor stores and are often sold as stands for large candles or marble cheese trays.

MATERIALS

- Marble disc 14in (35cm) in diameter and 1in (2.5cm) deep
- White pebbles approximately 1½in (4cm) long
- White cement-based adhesive
- Small pointed kitchen knife

step 1

If the marble disc is not new, wash and scrub it well to whiten it and remove any greasy dirt. Sort out similarly sized pebbles, trying to select those that have one flat side. Mix the cement to a fairly stiff consistency and spread on the back of each pebble before setting it into place around the rim of the disc. A little of the cement will squash out from underneath the pebble. Leave this for the moment to harden slightly.

step 2

Continue placing the pebbles all the way around the edge of the marble disc, then leave for 30 minutes or slightly longer until the cement is beginning to set. At this point slice off the excess cement with the knife and push extra in to fill any gaps. Make sure all excess cement is now removed from the pebbles. Allow to dry overnight before using the tray.

Table trivet

This practical table trivet looks as though it has been made with semi-precious stones such as agates, cornelians or amber. This is because the pebbles have been polished, which reveals and enhances the beautiful natural characteristics of the stones. They are not only lovely to look at but also feel remarkably smooth and cool to the touch.

Once the pebbles have been selected they are cemented into a shallow metal dish, for example, the kind that may be used to stand a large candle on. They have been grouted with black grout which creates a rich effect, with the dark stones glinting out of a dark background. Polished stones are relatively easy to obtain but they will be more expensive than those in their raw state, so it is sensible to use them for smaller projects. They would look rather spectacular laid as a surface on a small outdoor table. As always, once you feel confident with these techniques, you will invent more ambitious projects for yourself.

MATERIALS

- Cement-based adhesive
- Shallow metal dish 8in (20cm) in diameter
- 7 pale pebbles between 1½in (4cm) and 2in (5cm) long
- 15 assorted colored pebbles approx ½in (1cm) in diameter
- 20 red pebbles between ¾in (2cm) and 1½in (3cm) long
- Assorted small black pebbles
- Waterproof and frostproof cement-based black grout
- Palette knife
- Cloths

step **1**
Mix the cement adhesive to a fairly stiff consistency and evenly fill the shallow dish to a depth of ¼in (5mm).

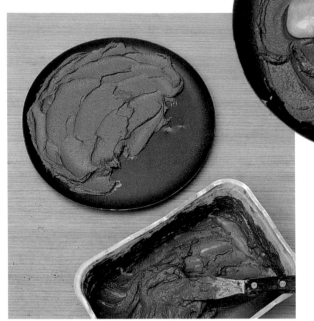

step **2**
Set the seven large pale-colored pebbles into the cement making a central flower shape, as in the picture. Make sure that the tops of the pebbles lie level with the top of the rim of the dish.

step **3**
Take eight of the smallest colored pebbles and set them into the cement in the center of the flower shape. Make sure that they are level with the larger pebbles, adding cement to the back of the pebbles as necessary.

step **4**
Take the 20 red pebbles and set them into the cement along the inside rim of the metal dish making a ring. Remember to keep the pebbles at the same level as all the others by adding cement to the back of the pebbles if need be.

step 5

Add seven of the smallest colored pebbles around the central flower shape, next to the outer ring of red pebbles, spacing them equally, as in the picture between the "petals." Fill in the remaining space within the circle with small black pebbles, ensuring that they are at the same level as the other pebbles. Leave to dry overnight.

step 6

Mix the grout according to the manufacturer's instructions and work it into the gaps between the pebbles with the palette knife. Remove the excess from the surface of the table trivet with a damp cloth. When the grout is dry, polish the finished table trivet with a dry cloth.

Mirror frame

This simple mirror frame evokes memories of the washed-out, natural shades of beach pebbles at low tide. Framed by faded green stones, the chalky bleached colors of the central pebbles make this an ideal mirror to display in a garden room, positioned perhaps on a limewashed wall.

The mirror could not be easier to make; the standard-size, round, mirrored glass panel and wooden back are designed to be used for mosaic work, while selected pebbles are placed into a pale cement adhesive which sets fairly quickly and is weatherproof. If you want to display the mirror outdoors throughout the year, simply treat the wooden frame with an exterior varnish.

You do not need to be too ambitious for this charming project – simple designs are the most effective for a truly striking effect in a smaller feature such as this.

MATERIALS

- Circular mirror 8in (20cm) in diameter
- MDF circular frame with rim 16in (40cm) in diameter
- Silicone adhesive
- Cement-based adhesive
- Container for cement
- Blue/green pebbles 1in (2.5cm) long
- White pebbles 1–1½in (2.5–4cm) long
- 7 blue/green pebbles over 1½in (4cm) long
- Pale green paint
- Paintbrush

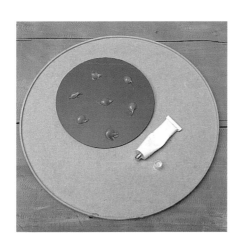

step *1*

Center the mirror on the circular MDF frame and with a pencil trace the outline. Using the silicone adhesive, stick the mirror onto the center of the circular MDF frame and allow to dry.

step *2*

Apply some cement around the edge of the mirror and set in the smaller blue/green pebbles, angled out so that they cover the joint.

step *3*

Set the remaining smaller blue/green pebbles around the outer rim, this time angling the pebbles outward to hide the edge of the MDF frame.

step *4*

Apply the cement to the area of the MDF still visible and set in the white pebbles, close together, between the two blue/green rings. Do one section of the frame at a time. Place the seven larger blue/green pebbles among the white pebbles, spaced equally around the circle. Allow to dry, then paint the outer rim of the MDF frame with the pale green paint.

Hurricane lanterns

Candles placed in hurricane lanterns are ideal for illuminating a garden table at night, as the tall glass cylinders protect the flames from the gentlest of breezes. The stone bases of these lanterns have been randomly decorated with an assortment of small colored pebbles. They have a chalky finish when dry, but if you would like to enhance and deepen their color, simply spray the finished base with a waterproof matt varnish.

After working for a while with a variety of pebbles in all colors, shapes and sizes, you will find yourself growing more fascinated by them, marveling at their myriad forms, never finding a double, choosing a favorite, saving it in your pocket, wondering about its origins. Such a simple activity can become wonderfully interesting and rather therapeutic. Children, in particular, love to sort, grade and size pebbles, an activity that can stimulate an interest in geology and the natural history of the world.

MATERIALS

- Bowl of small colored polished pebbles, ½-¾in (1-2cm) in diameter
- Gray cement-based adhesive
- Small pointed kitchen knife
- 2 hurricane lanterns with cylindrical stone bases, approximately 4in (10cm) in diameter and 3in (7.5cm) high

step 1

Sort the pebbles into similar sizes and a good variety of colors. It helps to evaluate them more clearly if they are wet.

step 2

Mix the cement to a fairly stiff consistency. Working on a quarter of the lantern base at a time, spread the cement onto the curved side of the base. Set the stones into place closely together, distributing different colors as evenly as possible. Make sure the pebbles at the top edge will not interfere with the fit of the glass in the stand.

step 3

Continue sticking the pebbles around the lantern base until all the surface is covered. Carefully clean off any excess cement, making sure that none is smeared on the pebbles and allow the cement to harden overnight before use.

Orchid saucer

This uncomplicated project has a really practical use. The bowl filled with water and sandblasted glass pebbles provides essential humidity for the beautiful orchid *Phalaenopsis*. In their natural environment, these orchids grow in trees in a humid jungle, their roots open to the air and light. This is why they are grown in transparent pots (opaque pots would mean the roots would work their way out toward the light). It is also important that these sensitive roots don't sit in water, so raising the pot on the bed of pebbles is ideal.

There are many other pot plants that warrant the same conditions; in fact, most would benefit from similar treatment, especially as they have to survive in the rather dry atmosphere of our centrally heated homes.

MATERIALS

- White cement-based waterproof adhesive
- Container for cement
- Palette knife
- Pale cream or white china flat-bottomed bowl, approximately 4in (10cm) high and 8in (20cm) in diameter
- 50 sandblasted lozenge-shaped pebbles, 1½–2in (4–5cm) in length

step *1*

Mix the cement according to the manufacturer's instructions and cover the base of the china bowl with a layer about ¾in (2cm) thick. Try to make the surface as smooth as possible, rather as you would do with cake batter.

step *2*

Set the pebbles firmly into the cement so that they are standing up on their ends and fit closely together.

step *3*

Continue setting the pebbles in until the base of the bowl is tightly packed. Allow the cement to dry for two days before pouring on water.

Acknowledgments

We owe a debt of gratitude to Nan Farquharson, Daniela Zimmerman and Jeremy Menuhin, as well as Jill Patchett and Alan Du Monceau, for allowing us to use their lovely gardens in which to take some of the photographs in the book. A very big thank you to Heini Schneebeli for letting us use his studio to work in, and to Mary White who jollied us along at difficult moments when we were flagging.

We would also like to thank our managing editor at Cico, Georgina Harris, who helped to run this project so smoothly; her enthusiasm and wit was much appreciated. Many thanks are due to Cindy Richards, our publisher, who commissioned the book knowing we would be the right combination of people to make it work, and lastly to Gillian Haslam, our wonderful behind-the-scenes editor.

The Publishers would like to thank The Edifice Picture Library for use of the photographs on pages 8–15.

All photographs on pages 8–15 Copyright © Edifice Picture Library: Sayer/Lewis/Mellis/Brown/Darley/Schneebeli